Transportation
Machines
At Work

Buses

By Hal Rogers

The Child's World®, Inc.

Published by The Child's World®, Inc.
PO Box 326
Chanhassen, MN 55317-0326
800-599-READ
www.childsworld.com

Design and Production:
The Creative Spark, San Juan Capistrano, CA

Photos: © 2000 David M. Budd Photography: cover, 5, 8–10, 13–17, 19, 21, 23
      © Kevin R. Morris/CORBIS: 6

We thank Colorado Charter Lines for their help in preparing this book.

Library of Congress Cataloging-in-Publication Data

Rogers, Hal, 1966-
      Buses / by Hal Rogers.
          p. cm.
      ISBN 1-56766-963-8
      1. Buses—Juvenile literature. [1. Buses.] I. Title.
TL232 .R64 2001
629.222'33—dc21

                                        00-011375

Contents

On the Job

On the job, buses carry people from place to place. They can carry many people at a time.

Students can ride a bus to school.

They can take a bus on field trips, too.

Some grown-ups ride a bus to work.

Others take a bus to the airport.

Passengers climb steps to **board**

a bus.

Bus drivers use a button or **lever** to open and close the door.

Bus passengers sit in the **cabin.** The cabin has lots of seats. This bus can carry many passengers. Its cabin has **bins** above the seats. The passengers can put small bags and packages in the bins.

This bus has storage bins underneath, too. Passengers can put suitcases in the bins. The bins have doors on both sides of the bus.

13

The bus has a large **windshield.** The driver looks through the windshield.

The bus also has outside mirrors.

These mirrors help the driver see

other **vehicles.**

Buses have big windows on

both sides.

Buses also have very big tires.

Climb Aboard!

Would you like to see where the bus driver sits? The driver uses a steering wheel and **controls** to drive the bus. The inside mirror lets the driver see passengers behind him. **Pedals** on the floor make the bus stop and go.

Up Close

The inside

1. The driver's seat

2. The steering wheel

3. The controls

4. The pedals

5. The bins

6. The passenger seats

The outside

1. The windows

2. The windshield

3. The mirrors

4. The door

5. The bins

6. The tires

Glossary

bins (BINZ)
Bins are places where people store things. A bus has bins inside its cabin.

board (BORD)
When people board a bus, they get on it. People use steps to board a bus.

cabin (KAB-in)
A cabin is the space inside a bus where passengers sit. A bus cabin has many seats.

controls (kun-TROLZ)
Controls are buttons, switches, and other tools that make a machine work. A bus driver uses controls to drive the bus.

lever (LEV-er)
A lever is a bar or handle used to make something work. A bus driver uses a lever to open the door.

passengers (PASS-en-jerz)
Passengers are travelers in vehicles such as buses, cars, trains, and airplanes. Passengers ride in the cabin of a bus.

pedals (PED-ulz)
Pedals are controls that people work with their feet. Pedals on the floor make a bus stop and go.

vehicles (VEE-hih-kulz)
Vehicles are machines that take people and things from place to place. Buses and cars are vehicles.

windshield (WIND-sheeld)
A windshield is a window on the front of a bus or car. Buses have a very large windshield.